Prescription for
RAISING TEENS

June H. Olin

Published by June H. Olin
PMB 120
2020 Fieldstone Parkway, Suite 900
Franklin, Tennessee 37069
Printed in the United States of America

Library of Congress Control Number 2005902324
ISBN 0-9767447-2-4

Scripture quotations are taken from and used by permission, all rights reserved: *The Amplified Bible* (AMP). *The Amplified Bible, Old Testament*. Copyright © 1965, 1987 by Zondervan Corporation. *The Amplified Bible, New Testament*, Copyright 1958, 1987 by the Lockman Foundation. ** *The Holy Bible, New International Version* (NIV). Copyright © 1973, 1978, 1984 by International Bible Society. Used by permission of Zondervan Publishing House. ** The Message (MSG) Copyright © 2002 by Eugene H. Patterson

** *The New King James Version* (NKJV). Copyright © 1982 by Thomas Nelson, Inc. ** *The Holy Bible, New Living Translation* (NLT) Copyright © 1996 Tyndale House Publishers, Inc. Wheaton, Illinois 60189. **Author's Note - In certain translations, some publishers have not capitalized pronouns referring to God and Jesus. We apologize for the confusion.**

ACKNOWLEDGMENTS

My sincere "thank you" to the many teenagers who took the time to share with me your inner-most thoughts and ideas. I also appreciate your honesty and forthrightness plus your insightful comments. Without your input, Rx for Raising Teens would just be like any other book. You have helped create a book based on truth. You have given teens across the country a voice, and parents direction and insights into your world. I firmly believe this book will act as a guideline for parents and will be instrumental in helping mend the family unit.

INTRODUCTION

I must begin by explaining my motivation for writing this Rx for Raising Teens book. I have been raising three teenagers for the past three years and I've had at least one teenager for the last seven years. I felt a need to pen a book based on 100 percent practice, throwing all theory out the window. I've learned more about this world and life in general from my teens. They have forced me to be candid with myself about my weaknesses because of their blatant honesty! I laugh while writing this because we all are candid and up front about our strengths and talents. We admit we have them and even revel in them at times. On the contrary, we flee from facing unpleasant truths about ourselves.

In an unprecedented notion, I felt led to base this book on "suggestions" from the teenagers themselves. The majority of "suggestions" in this book came directly from the "horse's mouth". I interviewed and e-mailed teens across the country asking them for advice to parents on Raising Teens. I asked the teen to put themselves in their parents' "shoes" and to give me several suggestions on how to effectively raise a "good, wholesome, well-rounded teenager" today. Interestingly, the teens were eager to give me their suggestions and at times were stricter than I expected.

Without giving away too much of the "meat" of this book, I will enlighten you parents on the teen's "Number one" suggestion across the board. It was, "listen to your child!" I will not elaborate on this now for it is intertwined throughout most of this book and is quite interesting. I'd hate to spoil the mystery of these informative, eye opening responses taken directly from our teens.

My intentions in writing this book are to bring about awareness, healing, restoration, renewal of relationships and much peace in the family unit. In order for this to be done, I had to be blatantly honest with you and share many of our family trials, tribulations, and blessed times as well. Keep in mind, what works for me will not always work for you. You must seek and ask for God's wisdom in raising your teens. He is the ultimate Authority and Parent. What I have to offer you is my seven years of experience in raising my teens. I have enjoyed and treasured the teenage years the most. My sons have become remarkable young men, and I am deeply honored to be called their "Mom". My desire is for you, too, to be proud and honored to be called "Mom" or "Dad" by your teen.

Enjoy this book and remember your teens provided the suggestions. "Listen" to them!

SUGGESTIONS

1- LISTEN
2- BE A HANDS-ON PARENT
3- OVERLOOK THE LITTLE THINGS
4- DISCIPLINE YOUR TEENS AND STICK WITH IT
5- HOME SHOULD BE A COMFORTABLE PEACEFUL ENVIRONMENT IN WHICH YOUR TEEN FEELS SAFE BRINGING FRIENDS
6- EMPATHIZE WITH THEM
7- GOD FIRST, FAMILY SECOND, JOBS AND EVERYTHING ELSE, AFTER THAT...
8- INVESTIGATE OTHER TEENS PERSONALLY
9- TRUST YOUR CHILD, BUT ALWAYS KEEP YOUR EYES WIDE OPEN
10- BE OPEN ENOUGH FOR YOUR TEEN TO FEEL COMFORTABLE TO TALK TO YOU ABOUT ANYTHING
11- BE JUST CRAZY ENOUGH TO BE THE "EXCUSE" YOUR CHILD USES FOR SAYING "NO"
12- BAND TOGETHER WITH OTHER PARENTS OF TEENAGERS
13- ATTEND CHURCH WITH YOUR TEENS
14- BE AWAKE AT NIGHT WHEN YOUR TEEN GETS HOME
15- KEEP YOUR ALCOHOL CONSUMPTION TO A BARE MINIMUM AROUND YOUR CHILDREN

SUGGESTIONS

16- Frequently Read And Discuss The Bible With Your Teen

17- Find The Right School

18- Don't Allow Any Back Talk

19- Require Your Teen To Get A Part-Time Job

20- Monitor What Your Child Watches And Reads

21- Periodically, Drive By Where They Are Supposed To Be

22- Talk To Your Child About Abstinence

23- Don't Give Up On Your Child They Are Never Too Far Gone

24- Ask For Forgiveness, And Forgive

25- Stay On Your Knees In Constant Prayer For Your Child

26- Walk Your Talk

27- Minimize Your Phone Calls Once Your Teen gets Home

28- Find Others Who Have Successfully Raised Teenagers; Listen And Learn From Them

29- Convince Your Teen To Join A Church Youth Group

30- Provide Good Solid Family Time On A Regular Basis

31- Keep Tabs On Your Teen's Homework Assignments

32- Do Not Allow Your Teen To Hang Out With The "Wrong" Crowd

SUGGESTIONS

33- LEAD BY EXAMPLE

34- SHOW AFFECTION

35- USE EVERY OPPORTUNITY TO TEACH YOUR CHILD LIFE SKILLS

36- CALL THEM OFTEN WHEN THEY ARE OUT

37- STAY COOL EVEN WHEN YOUR TEEN PROVOKES YOU OTHERWISE

38- BE AVAILABLE WHEN THEY WANT TO TALK - EVEN AT YOUR MOST INCONVENIENT TIMES

39- ADMIT YOUR TEEN CAN DO WRONG

40- ALLOW YOUR TEEN TO EXPRESS THEIR OPINIONS, WITHOUT PARENTAL JUDGMENT

41- HAVE YOUR TEEN ALTERNATE SLEEPOVERS FROM THEIR FRIENDS' HOMES TO YOUR HOME

42- KEEP YOUR TEEN INVOLVED

43- RESPECT YOUR TEEN

44- ROUTINELY SCHEDULE ONE-ON-ONE TIME WITH YOUR CHILD

45- MAKE YOUR TEEN SIT WITH OR NEAR YOU AT CHURCH

46- BE HOME WHEN YOUR TEEN GETS HOME FROM SCHOOL OR WORK

47- KEEP YOUR PRIORITIES STRAIGHT

48- BE A STRICT PARENT WITHOUT OVERDOING IT

49- MEET AND GET TO KNOW THEIR FRIENDS

50- ENCOURAGE, ENCOURAGE, ENCOURAGE

PRAYER NOTES
for a
NEW BEGINNING

Today, God's Word spoke this to me_____

_____

_____

_____

_____

I will let go of_____

_____

_____

_____

_____

I will begin by_____

_____

_____

_____

¹⁹**My dear brothers and sisters, be quick to listen, slow to speak, and slow to get angry.**

James 1:19 (NLT)

This recommendation was given consistently by all teens polled as their Number one suggestion. The listening that they are suggesting here is really hearing what your teen is saying, not just sitting and daydreaming about something else while they're talking. It's also respecting their opinions even though they are different than yours. We want the Lord to hear our prayer and listen to us. Under that same token your teen needs and desires that same understanding and attention from you. Please let them finish what they are saying, even when you are churning inside to respond.

Remember, this was their Number one suggestion for you. Actively listen to your teen!

PRAYER NOTES
for a
NEW BEGINNING

Today, God's Word spoke this to me_____

_____

_____

_____

_____

_____

I will let go of_____

_____

_____

_____

_____

I will begin by_____

_____

_____

_____

_____

²⁷She keeps an eye on everyone in her household, and keeps them all busy and productive.

²⁸ Her children respect and bless her; her husband joins in with words of praise:

Proverbs 31: 27-28 (MSG)

If you are not already active in your teen's life, begin by taking baby steps and get involved. For instance, my husband travels often and my 15-year-old son has a passion for baseball. He and I spend three days a week at a batting cage. Outside the cage I stand calling out "hit it to left field, hit it up the middle, bunt it down the line, etc." I am actively involved in every aspect of his batting practice.

I grew up so feminine, it was almost sickening. I knew absolutely nothing about baseball until my sons showed an interest. I learned the sport to the point of even becoming my son's coach. Please take the time to learn your child's passion.

This is just one example of many hands-on activities we share as a family. By immersing yourself in your child's life, you are helping create in them a strong sense of self worth. Hands-on means, "I'm interested in you."

PRAYER NOTES
for a
NEW BEGINNING

Today, God's Word spoke this to me_____

_____

_____

_____

_____

I will let go of_____

_____

_____

_____

_____

I will begin by_____

_____

_____

_____

> ¹¹People with good sense restrain their anger; they earn esteem by overlooking wrongs.
>
> **Proverbs 19:11 (NLT)**

My grandmother raised four children. She once told me when I was at wits' end with my children, "June, if I spanked my kids for everything they did wrong, I would have killed them." In other words, you must overlook many of the little things and by doing this; you are teaching them God's grace.

PRAYER NOTES
for a
NEW BEGINNING

Today, God's Word spoke this to me_____
_____
_____
_____
_____
_____

I will let go of_____
_____
_____
_____
_____
_____

I will begin by_____
_____
_____
_____

²⁴**A refusal to correct is a refusal to love; love your children by disciplining them.**

Proverbs 13:24 (MSG)

Inconsistent discipline is worse than no discipline at all. If your child does not know there are definite ramifications to their actions, they will be more apt to disrespect your authority.

While I was receiving my bachelors degree in criminology, I learned the three tenets of the deterrence theory. Punishment must be swift, severe and certain in order for it to work. This means reacting immediately to the offense and taking away something of value to them when they disobey.

If you are guilty of being passive with your child in the past, don't concentrate on what you didn't do, but put your efforts on a fresh start today. Take into account what God's Word says; a firm hand is a sign of love to your child!

See also all of Hebrews 12

PRAYER NOTES
for a
NEW BEGINNING

Today, God's Word spoke this to me_____

_____

_____

_____

_____

I will let go of_____

_____

_____

_____

_____

I will begin by_____

_____

_____

_____

_____

> ¹⁸If it is possible, as far as it depends on you, live at peace with everyone.
>
> **Romans 12:18 (NIV)**

For ten years, our home has been the ping-pong capital of our teen's school. We use a $10 ping-pong table purchased at a yard sale, continue to keep a well-stocked refrigerator, always rent videos, and give them ample space. Please understand staying out of their way does not mean no supervision. It means pleasantly meeting and greeting their friends, spending some time getting to know them, and then giving them room. One more word of wisdom. Do more listening than you do talking.

A few thought-provoking questions may earn you some interesting insights regarding your child.

PRAYER NOTES
for a
NEW BEGINNING

Today, God's Word spoke this to me_____

_____

_____

_____

_____

I will let go of_____

_____

_____

_____

_____

_____

I will begin by_____

_____

_____

_____

6. Empathize With Them

⁸**And above all things have fervent love for one another, for "love will cover a multitude of sins."**
1 Peter 4:8 (NKJV)

I've watched too many parents break a child's spirit by being too demanding and insensitive. Think back to your teenage years and the many trials and issues you encountered. Before making a harsh judgment on your child, filter it through your own teenage experiences. Hopefully, this will shed some light on your teenager's perspective. If your teen knows they don't have to live up to overly lofty standards, then they are more likely to open up and communicate with you. Love your child for who they are, regardless of how different that might be from you.

PRAYER NOTES
for a
NEW BEGINNING

Today, God's Word spoke this to me_____

_____

_____

_____

_____

I will let go of_____

_____

_____

_____

_____

I will begin by_____

_____

_____

_____

⁴He must manage his own family well and see that his children obey him with proper respect.
⁵(If anyone does not know how to manage his own family, how can he take care of God's church?)

1 Timothy 3:4-5 (NIV)

My dear parent, when your priorities get scrambled, you are like a soda machine with an "out of order" sign taped on the front. God is very plain and direct when teaching priorities. If just one gets "out of whack," all the rest suffer!

For instance, Dads, how does your work and career fit into your priorities? How about that Saturday golf outing versus spending time playing catch with your son? Moms, the same goes for you. If you are overextended in any area of your life, your family and relationship with God is negatively affected.

If your priorities are "out of order," then I implore you to start today by saying "No" to others and "Yes" to God and family!

23

PRAYER NOTES
for a
NEW BEGINNING

Today, God's Word spoke this to me_____

_____

_____

_____

_____

I will let go of_____

_____

_____

_____

_____

I will begin by_____

_____

_____

_____

²⁰Become wise by walking with the wise;
hang out with fools and watch
your life fall to pieces.

Proverbs 13:20 (MSG)

The term investigate is extremely accurate here. Investigation involves using multiple sources. Don't just use hearsay from other parents, but go to the horse's mouths (which are the teens themselves). For example, when you and your teen are in a casual game of ping-pong or out on a shopping spree, inquire as to what "Sally" is like. For example, what are "Sally's" interests? What kind of girl is she? Just a few simple questions and an acute listening ear, could bring about a wealth of truths.

PRAYER NOTES
for a
NEW BEGINNING

Today, God's Word spoke this to me_____

_____

_____

_____

_____

I will let go of_____

_____

_____

_____

_____

I will begin by_____

_____

_____

_____

¹⁶I am sending you out like sheep among wolves. Therefore be as shrewd as snakes and as innocent as doves.

Matthew 10:16 (NIV)

According to this Scripture, we are to use God's discerning wisdom in raising our children, and at the same time, maintain a level of trust in them. Let them spread their wings while always keeping a watchful eye on where they are flying. Remember, even the most proficient flier sometimes encounters turbulence. Make sure when this occurs, you are there to take control.

PRAYER NOTES
for a
NEW BEGINNING

Today, God's Word spoke this to me_____

_____

_____

_____

_____

I will let go of_____

_____

_____

_____

_____

I will begin by_____

_____

_____

_____

_____

⁶Let your speech always be with grace, seasoned with salt, that you may know how you ought to answer each one.

Colossians 4:6 (NKJV)

Our three teens are extremely open with us. On numerous occasions, parents have stated to us, "Wow, your kids talk to you a lot. Our teen doesn't say anything." I firmly believe the reason our three teens are more open than most is solely because of our reactions to what they tell us.

A very important issue in listening to your teen is to remain cool and calm when your teen discloses something that shocks you. If you respond inappropriately, you risk them closing the lines of communication. Believe me, you want your teen talking to you rather than to somebody else who may be from an ungodly persuasion.

See Romans 15:7, 1 Peter 4:8

PRAYER NOTES
for a
NEW BEGINNING

Today, God's Word spoke this to me_____

_____

_____

_____

_____

_____

I will let go of_____

_____

_____

_____

_____

_____

I will begin by_____

_____

_____

_____

_____

> ⁹"Fight as you never have before, Philistines! If you don't, we will become the Hebrews' slaves just as they have been ours!"

1 Samuel 4:9 (NLT)

When our oldest child was entering high school, we went to a mandatory drug and alcohol prevention class, and learned invaluable advice on keeping our teens "clean". One of the instructor's top suggestions was extremely important. He stated that your child needs to know that they can use you as their excuse to say "No." Something that the instructor's teenager had stated profoundly stood out to me. She said "Dad, I hated it when I got to college because I could no longer use you as my excuse for saying no." Simply put, we should be the radical enough parent that would regularly check on our teens, casually question their intentions, and get to know their friends and their parents. By being the "crazy" parent, you have become the perfect excuse your child can use!

PRAYER NOTES
for a
NEW BEGINNING

Today, God's Word spoke this to me_____

_____

_____

_____

_____

I will let go of_____

_____

_____

_____

_____

I will begin by_____

_____

_____

_____

> ⁹We work together as partners who belong to God. You are God's field, God's building — not ours.

1 Corinthians 3:9 (NLT)

Try to steer your teen to friends whose parents have the same moral fiber as you. In this way, when your teen is at their friend's house, you have a compatriot keeping their eyes on your teen as well. In addition, many of the issues your teen will go through are the same as other teens. To have a consortium of parents working through these issues is exactly what God was talking about in this Scripture. Strength is in numbers, so find a good set of parent-friends.

PRAYER NOTES
for a
NEW BEGINNING

Today, God's Word spoke this to me_____

_____

_____

_____

_____

I will let go of_____

_____

_____

_____

_____

I will begin by_____

_____

_____

_____

> ¹Unless the LORD builds a house,
> the work of the builders is useless.
> Unless the LORD protects a city,
> guarding it with sentries will do no good.
>
> **Psalm 127:1 (NLT)**

I have seen too often where parents drop their teens off at church and leave. I am convinced that we are to lead by example, and if your teen wants to go to church, this is a huge positive step towards a relationship with God and a positive relationship with you. So go, give up your morning coffee or golf time, and gain an incredible relationship with God and your child.

PRAYER NOTES
for a
NEW BEGINNING

Today, God's Word spoke this to me _____
_____
_____
_____
_____

I will let go of _____
_____
_____
_____
_____

I will begin by _____
_____
_____
_____

> ³He will not let you stumble
> and fall; the one who watches
> over you will not sleep.
>
> **Psalm 121:3 (NLT)**

The notion of an alert parent being awake holds your teen accountable after their evening out. Also, sometimes you can have the most intimate conversations at this time of the night with your teen. Maybe it's because they're tired and their guard is down. Maybe it is because you are awake and they appreciate that you are available to hear about their evening exploits! I'm not sure why, but I do know that I have had many of my most treasured conversations with my teens after their evening out.

PRAYER NOTES
for a
NEW BEGINNING

Today, God's Word spoke this to me_____

_____

_____

_____

_____

I will let go of_____

_____

_____

_____

_____

I will begin by_____

_____

_____

_____

¹³**If what I eat is going to make another Christian sin, I will never eat meat again as long as I live — for I don't want to make another Christian stumble.**

1 Corinthians 8:13
(NLT)

If your teen is a believer in Jesus Christ, she is still considered a less mature believer than you. If you are drinking around your teen, no matter how infrequent, you could be a stumbling block for them. You may not have any difficulty with alcohol, and it may be absolutely meaningless to you, but as a parent, your first priority must be your child. We have found that abstaining completely from alcohol gives us that impetus to create a foundation in which alcohol is not a part of their lives, even when they become of drinking age.

PRAYER NOTES
for a
NEW BEGINNING

Today, God's Word spoke this to me_____

_____

_____

_____

_____

I will let go of_____

_____

_____

_____

_____

I will begin by_____

_____

_____

_____

¹⁶All Scripture is God-breathed and is useful for teaching, rebuking, correcting and training in righteousness, ¹⁷so that the man of God may be thoroughly equipped for every good work.

2 Timothy 3:16-17 (NIV)

We established a tradition early on in our children's upbringing to read the Bible with them every day before school. It became as regular as breakfast. Currently, we've had difficulty getting our daily Bible reading in because of time restraints. We found we were spending 10 minutes each morning on Bible reading, which allowed us no time for discussion or prayer. We quickly realized that this "fast food" devotion time had become ineffective. We have revamped our Bible studies to Friday mornings with a 45 minute time frame. This allows us coffee and hot chocolate, Bible reading, discussions and prayer time. This means that once a week, the kids will get up earlier, but their gain will be invaluable.

PRAYER NOTES
for a
NEW BEGINNING

Today, God's Word spoke this to me_____

_____

_____

_____

_____

I will let go of_____

_____

_____

_____

_____

I will begin by_____

_____

_____

_____

17. Find The Right School

> *"Train up a child in the way he should go, And when he is old he will not depart from it.*
>
> **Proverbs 22:6 (NKJV)**

No matter what your financial position, don't be boxed into believing you must have your teen go to the public school nearest you. Financial aid is available in most private Christian schools, and I have never seen a family turned away from a school they wanted to attend. Visit many schools in your town and ask questions about the school's biblical foundation, class size, test scores, and student-teacher ratios. Find other parents and students who attend the school, and ask them their opinions.

After moving 13 times, and having our children attend numerous public and private schools, I can tell you first hand that the private Christian schools my children have attended were far and above safer and exposed my teens to less drugs and premarital sex than the public schools. Most importantly, Jesus Christ was talked about in the hallways, classrooms, sporting events and everywhere else. We believe so much in this, that my husband commutes over 600 miles each week for work just so our children can remain in the Christian school.

PRAYER NOTES
for a
NEW BEGINNING

Today, God's Word spoke this to me_____

_____

_____

_____

_____

I will let go of_____

_____

_____

_____

_____

I will begin by_____

_____

_____

_____

²³Keep your heart with all diligence,
For out of it spring the issues of life.
²⁴Put away from you a deceitful mouth,
And put perverse lips far from you.

Proverbs 4:23-24 (NKJV)

One of our teens gave us more difficulty with back talk than the others. Coupled with the punishment he received for his disrespect, I also would give him pertinent Scriptures concerning what God said about his back talk and insolence. Strangely enough, the Scriptures quieted his ugly words and helped calm the situation. I found that God's Word, more so than my own words, were convicting to my son's heart. Again, we used God's Word coupled with discipline to eliminate his disrespect. One last point - Always rise above what's being said to you, and keep your cool. Otherwise, you will lose your effectiveness.

PRAYER NOTES
for a
NEW BEGINNING

Today, God's Word spoke this to me_____

_____

_____

_____

_____

I will let go of_____

_____

_____

_____

_____

I will begin by_____

_____

_____

_____

> ¹¹Hard work means prosperity;
> only fools idle away their time.
>
> **Proverbs 12:11 (NLT)**

When our first two teens turned 16, we required them to secure a part-time job to teach them responsibility. We're financially blessed enough that none of our children have to work. With their part-time job, we expect them to pay for their gas and entertainment. We have witnessed our children learn to budget their money and tithe just by giving them these responsibilities. Our middle son recently received a stellar employee review and was the only staff member to receive a raise. This taught him that having a good work ethic is of utmost importance. So even if you are capable of providing all their wants and needs, do not be lulled into thinking that your teen should not work. What they learn is invaluable and priceless.

PRAYER NOTES
for a
NEW BEGINNING

Today, God's Word spoke this to me_____

_____

_____

_____

_____

I will let go of_____

_____

_____

_____

_____

I will begin by_____

_____

_____

_____

20. MONITOR WHAT YOUR CHILD WATCHES AND READS

⁸**Finally, brothers, whatever is true, whatever is noble, whatever is right, whatever is pure, whatever is lovely, whatever is admirable - if anything is excellent or praiseworthy - think about such things.**

Philippians 4:8 (NIV)

Whether it's TV, computer, movies, books or magazines, keep a close eye on the content, and always put it to the Philippians 4:8 test. Is the content true, noble, pure, and admirable? Some cable companies will block channels at your request. Use www.screenit.com to investigate movies. Plus, take the time to preview all reading materials. Don't simply accept what other teens are doing as appropriate for your child. Research it yourself and you decide.

PRAYER NOTES
for a
NEW BEGINNING

Today, God's Word spoke this to me_____

_____

_____

_____

_____

I will let go of_____

_____

_____

_____

_____

I will begin by_____

_____

_____

_____

21. PERIODICALLY, DRIVE BY WHERE THEY ARE SUPPOSED TO BE

⁵**If you need wisdom — if you want to know what God wants you to do — ask him, and he will gladly tell you. He will not resent your asking.**

James 1:5 (NLT)

Please don't get your feathers ruffled. I'm not telling you to distrust your child. I am recommending you be a smart parent and keep tabs on your teen. You're responsible to parent your child. Your teen should always know that if the Holy Spirit lays on your heart that something is not adding up, you will get in your car in a heartbeat and investigate the situation.

PRAYER NOTES
for a
NEW BEGINNING

Today, God's Word spoke this to me_____

_____

_____

_____

_____

I will let go of_____

_____

_____

_____

_____

I will begin by_____

_____

_____

_____

⁸Now I say to those who aren't married and to widows — it's better to stay unmarried, just as I am.
⁹But if they can't control themselves, they should go ahead and marry.
It's better to marry than to burn with lust.

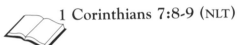

1 Corinthians 7:8-9 (NLT)

Parents usually cringe when they hear this subject and run away from broaching the matter with their teen.

I've always been extremely open and matter-of-fact when approaching the subject of sex. I firmly believe that by my not avoiding the topic and my ease in talking it over with my sons, I have created a relaxed "sex-talk" atmosphere. Because I am comfortable in broaching this subject with my teen boys, I have spent as much time as my husband addressing this issue. Don't get hung up on who will talk to them. Just do it! One or both of you; it really doesn't matter. Talk very matter-of-fact. Explain the consequences of premarital sex and what God says about it. Tell them how God has given us the incredible gift of sex once we are married. Give them suggestions on how to abstain. You can do it. I did and still do!

Your teen will probably resist your talking about sex, so approach the subject slowly and ever-so carefully, similar to the way you'd drink a cup of piping hot coffee…one sip at a time.

PRAYER NOTES
for a
NEW BEGINNING

Today, God's Word spoke this to me_____

_____

_____

_____

_____

I will let go of_____

_____

_____

_____

_____

I will begin by_____

_____

_____

_____

²¹Words kill, words give life;
they're either poison or fruit —you
choose.

Proverbs 18:21 (MSG)

Dear parents, please refrain from berating your teen or telling others what a disappointment they have become. Instead, infuse your child with God's Word. Take a couple of Scriptures from this book or from your Bible, insert your child's name in it, pray and speak **out loud** *these verses daily. By doing this, you are literally speaking eternal life into your child. Close your eyes to your child's circumstances, and open your eyes and mouth to God's truths. By placing your trust in Him, you will never give up, because you can rest in the fact that God is in control. Your responsibility is controlling your tongue, and he'll take care of the rest.*

See Galatians 6:9

PRAYER NOTES
for a
NEW BEGINNING

Today, God's Word spoke this to me_____

_____

_____

_____

_____

_____

I will let go of _____

_____

_____

_____

_____

_____

I will begin by_____

_____

_____

_____

²⁵"And when you stand praying,
if you hold anything against anyone,
forgive him, so that your Father in heaven
may forgive you your sins."

Mark 11:25-26 (NIV)

There have been times when my children have been disrespectful, and agitated me to the point where I lost my temper and said things that I didn't mean. This is where you as a parent must make the decision on doing what's right, and apologize to your child without excuses and ask them to forgive you. By doing this, you are teaching your child how to humble themselves and admit when they are wrong. Basically, they will not learn this concept of forgiveness except by watching your actions.

Remember the scenario, my teen was the first to do wrong, yet I was the first to humble myself and ask my teen for forgiveness. In doing so, my responsibility as a parent kicked in, and I became the example my teen needed.

PRAYER NOTES
for a
NEW BEGINNING

Today, God's Word spoke this to me_____

_____

_____

_____

_____

I will let go of_____

_____

_____

_____

_____

I will begin by_____

_____

_____

_____

_____

³"Call to Me, and I will answer you, and show you great and mighty things, which you do not know."

Jeremiah 33:3 (NKJV)

Our family prays together every morning before leaving for school and work. We have been doing this for years! My husband and I also pray together every night for our children before we go to sleep. Not only should you partner with someone in prayer, but I encourage you to be in constant prayer for your child. 1 Thessalonian 5:17 says "pray without ceasing."

I know prayer changes lives, so let it begin to change yours!

PRAYER NOTES
for a
NEW BEGINNING

Today, God's Word spoke this to me_____

_____

_____

_____

_____

I will let go of_____

_____

_____

_____

_____

I will begin by_____

_____

_____

_____

¹⁸Dear children, let us not love
with words or tongue
but with actions and in truth.

1 John 3:18 (NIV)

What's your response when an irate driver cuts you off? How do you handle yourself when a sales clerk is rude? How do you talk to your spouse on a regular basis? Are you the first in line offering to help people when a need arises? Don't forget that your children's eyes are on you at all times. How you act is what they will become. You know the saying, "Actions speak louder than words." Your actions will always speak louder to your child than anything you say to them.

PRAYER NOTES
for a
NEW BEGINNING

Today, God's Word spoke this to me_____

_____

_____

_____

_____

I will let go of_____

_____

_____

_____

_____

I will begin by_____

_____

_____

_____

27. MINIMIZE YOUR PHONE CALLS ONCE YOUR TEEN GETS HOME

⁴Show me Your ways, O LORD;
Teach me Your paths.
⁵Lead me in Your truth and teach me,
For You are the God of my salvation;
On You I wait all the day.

Psalm 25:4-5 (NKJV)

Utilize your free time to make personal and business phone calls when your teen is either gone to school, work, or over to a friend's house. Strive to be available when they are home, just in case they might want to "open up" to you. Don't make your child share you with the telephone, TV, or even a book. Even though your child is a teen, they need you more now, in the sense of listening to them, supporting them, and providing structure, than even when they were younger. Teenage issues and problems are overwhelming today; therefore you should make every effort to be available when the opportunity presents itself.

PRAYER NOTES
for a
NEW BEGINNING

Today, God's Word spoke this to me_____

_____

_____

_____

_____

I will let go of_____

_____

_____

_____

_____

I will begin by_____

_____

_____

_____

³Likewise, teach the older women to be reverent in the way they live, not to be slanderers or addicted to much wine, but to teach what is good.
⁴Then they can train the younger women to love their husbands and children,
⁵to be self-controlled and pure, to be busy at home, to be kind, and to be subject to their husbands, so that no one will malign the word of God.

Titus 2:3-5 (NIV)

Outside of my parents, I never really searched for a mentor, because I didn't know where to begin. It is important to get a different perspective on child rearing than just the way you were raised. Books are great, but the ability to have that one-on-one mentoring and personal prayer time with a wise Godly family can be invaluable.

In your church, actively search for seasoned parents, by joining bible studies, small groups or even getting involved in a mentoring program. Pray and ask God to lead you to a family who has already raised their children and can offer you Godly advice, support and prayer.

PRAYER NOTES
for a
NEW BEGINNING

Today, God's Word spoke this to me_____

_____

_____

_____

_____

I will let go of_____

_____

_____

_____

_____

I will begin by_____

_____

_____

_____

²⁴Let's see how inventive we can be in
encouraging love and helping out,
²⁵not avoiding worshiping together as some
do but spurring each other on, especially as
we see the big Day approaching.

Hebrews 10: 24-25 (MSG)

Don't take "no" for an answer. Being a member of a church youth group should be one of your mandatory rules. Your child will be meeting and spending time with other Christian teens plus they will learn how to praise and worship God from people geared towards the teenage generation.

Don't get hung up on where they are going to youth group. For example, our children attend youth group at a different church than where we are members. They have met wonderful Christian friends and are led by a caring Christian youth team. Always urge your child to "hang out" with other Christians.

PRAYER NOTES
for a
NEW BEGINNING

Today, God's Word spoke this to me_____

_____

_____

_____

_____

I will let go of_____

_____

_____

_____

_____

I will begin by_____

_____

_____

_____

30. PROVIDE GOOD SOLID FAMILY TIME ON A REGULAR BASIS

¹⁰I appeal to you, brothers, in the name of our Lord Jesus Christ, that all of you agree with one another so that there may be no divisions among you and that you may be perfectly united in mind and thought.

1 Corinthians 1:10 (NIV)

During the Spring, Summer and Fall months, my family eats dinner together almost every evening on our back porch. We sit and watch the birds build their nests in the Spring, feed their babies in the Summer, and fly away in the Fall. The outdoors seems to provide a very relaxing atmosphere for our children to share some of their daily activities. Ironically, my three teenagers and husband balked at eating outside because they complained, "It's too hot." "It's too cold." "It's too this....it's too that...." But I dug my heels in and forced the issue. Our outdoor dinners are filled with laughter, sharing and sometimes even a few food fights (can't do that inside!).

Make your family time fun and a little wacky. Remember, your teen comes from a completely different era than you. So at times, get on their silly, crazy level whether it be wrestling, playing practical jokes, or even a game of charades. Keep your family time light, airy and fun.

69

PRAYER NOTES
for a
NEW BEGINNING

Today, God's Word spoke this to me _____

_____

_____

_____

_____

I will let go of _____

_____

_____

_____

_____

I will begin by _____

_____

_____

_____

31. KEEP TABS ON YOUR TEEN'S HOMEWORK ASSIGNMENTS

³Through wisdom a house is built,
And by understanding it is established.

Proverbs 24:3 (NKJV)

Our youngest son has always loved to learn. Every teacher that taught him in elementary school and the early years of middle school bragged on his desire to gain more knowledge. He even read text books on history and wars, just for fun.

A metamorphosis occurred. He became a teenager. No more reading or studying. And no more passionate interest in learning. This is extremely common in teenagers. The school interest is overridden by their new interest in girls, cars and video games. For this reason, you must consistently check to see if they have completed their homework assignments, studied for an upcoming test, and finished school projects. If your school does not have a mechanism to let you know about your child's work assignments, meet with the teachers and create one yourself. This way, you stay actively involved. Inspect, rather than expect!

PRAYER NOTES
for a
NEW BEGINNING

Today, God's Word spoke this to me_____

_____

_____

_____

_____

I will let go of_____

_____

_____

_____

_____

I will begin by_____

_____

_____

_____

> ³³Do not be misled: "Bad company corrupts good character."
>
> **1 Corinthians 15:33 (NIV)**

No matter what it takes, get your teens away from other teenagers whose parents are not on the same "page" as you. For instance, we had a situation with one of our teenagers where he began developing a close friendship with a teen whose parents were more permissive than us. We noticed our teen becoming rebellious because he had limitations and his friend did not. And what went from a good relationship with our son became a battle just because of one friend. Through prayer we made the extremely difficult decision to stop the friendship. Granted this decision was not met with approval by anyone (our son, his friend or his friend's parents), but in standing up, taking the heat and doing what was right for our child, we gained a respectful son again. Please, if there is one thing I can get across to you; your responsibility is to raise YOUR child.

Sometimes you are going to have to choose your child's welfare over a friendship with another set of parents. Scripture makes it clear; we are here to please God, not man.

PRAYER NOTES
for a
NEW BEGINNING

Today, God's Word spoke this to me_____

_____

_____

_____

_____

_____

I will let go of_____

_____

_____

_____

_____

_____

I will begin by_____

_____

_____

_____

_____

33. LEAD BY EXAMPLE

⁷In everything set them an example by doing what is good. In your teaching show integrity, seriousness ⁸and soundness of speech that cannot be condemned, so that those who oppose you may be ashamed because they have nothing bad to say about us.

Titus 2:7-8 (NIV)

Our children are very generous with their possessions. They have watched us give to people since they were babies. Once our oldest son spent the night at a friend's house. He came home concerned for the family because the home was overrun with bugs and the family had very little money. Immediately, we called our exterminator, had them spray the family's house at our expense, and ask the company not to divulge our name. This blessed them and consequently taught our son the importance of responding to other's needs. We've provided for others on a very regular basis all our children's lives, and now we see the fruits of our efforts. Our teens are generous to others and the first to offer a helping hand!

PRAYER NOTES
for a
NEW BEGINNING

Today, God's Word spoke this to me_____

_____

_____

_____

_____

_____

I will let go of_____

_____

_____

_____

_____

I will begin by_____

_____

_____

_____

34. SHOW AFFECTION

⁴Love is patient, love is kind. It does not envy, it does not boast, it is not proud. ⁵It is not rude, it is not self-seeking, it is not easily angered, it keeps no record of wrongs. ⁶Love does not delight in evil but rejoices with the truth. ⁷It always protects, always trusts, always hopes, always perseveres.

 1 Corinthians 13:4-7 (NIV)

We're pretty wacky when it comes to showing affection. It's probably the strongest point in our family. When we watch TV together, you can find me lying beside my teenage sons, them lying in my lap, with me scratching their backs, or us just sitting there holding hands. But what you'll never find is us watching a movie together without me touching one, if not all four of my children. With regard to my daughter (my non-teen), you can find her curled up in my husband's lap. My very favorite thing I do with her is "snuggle piggy". "Snuggle piggy" in our family means we get into bed with our pajamas on, turn on something silly on TV, and snuggle. Showing affection is important to do to all of your children, and especially to the children of the opposite sex. Research has shown this is where they find their security and self esteem. Give your child a good, long hug today.

Note: showing affection has to include touching!

PRAYER NOTES
for a
NEW BEGINNING

Today, God's Word spoke this to me_____

_____

_____

_____

_____

I will let go of_____

_____

_____

_____

_____

I will begin by_____

_____

_____

_____

35. USE EVERY OPPORTUNITY TO TEACH YOUR CHILD LIFE SKILLS

⁵Love the LORD your God with all your heart and with all your soul and with all your strength. ⁶These commandments that I give you today are to be upon your hearts. ⁷Impress them on your children. Talk about them when you sit at home and when you walk along the road, when you lie down and when you get up.

Deuteronomy 6:5-7 (NIV)

As parents, whether you like it or not, you are teaching your child "life" on a daily basis. Rather than simply saying "yes" or "no" to them, couple your response with an explanation. Describe why things are done a certain way. When I was teaching my three teens how to drive, I used the opportunity as we sat at red lights to give them scenarios of possible harmful situations, also explaining how they should handle that situation should it occur. In addition to teaching driving skills, I have also addressed such issues as dating, work ethic, budgeting money, and most importantly their relationship with God. Remember, you are their most influential teacher. Use this short period of time to teach them what YOU want them to know. If you choose not to, someone less desirable could.

PRAYER NOTES
for a
NEW BEGINNING

Today, God's Word spoke this to me_____

_____

_____

_____

_____

_____

I will let go of_____

_____

_____

_____

_____

_____

I will begin by_____

_____

_____

_____

> ¹⁵The gullible believe anything they're told; the prudent sift and weigh every word.
>
> **Proverbs 14:15 (MSG)**

This suggestion came directly from one of our teens. He stated that because of our numerous phone calls, and his expectations that we were going to call, it kept him on the "straight and narrow". He gave the example that if a teen knows that his parent will be calling on a regular basis, the teen would be less likely to be getting into trouble. His reasoning was that a well placed phone call during the teen's misbehavior would force the teen to have to lie to the parents. Therefore, it would create two wrongs rather than just one.

I'm not saying to be a nuisance. I'm just suggesting that you be a presence while they're away from you.

PRAYER NOTES
for a
NEW BEGINNING

Today, God's Word spoke this to me_____

_____

_____

_____

_____

_____

I will let go of_____

_____

_____

_____

_____

_____

I will begin by_____

_____

_____

_____

_____

37. STAY COOL EVEN WHEN YOUR TEEN PROVOKES YOU OTHERWISE

> ¹A gentle answer turns away wrath, but a harsh word stirs up anger.
>
> **Proverbs 15:1 (NIV)**

There was a period when one of our sons was disrespectful. He knew how to push every single "button" to agitate my husband. I noticed my husband moving from the parental role to the role of an equal with his son. When this occurred, our teen's disrespect heightened. I brought to my husband's attention the damage that was occurring. Once he got a grip on the situation and moved back into his rightful parental role, the disrespect lessened and their relationship began to heal.

In order to keep your cool, here are a couple of suggestions.

1) Rise above what is being said to you and do not take it personal.

2) Discipline them immediately for any disrespect. If you can keep these two in check, the relationship will flourish.

See 1 Peter 3:8-9

PRAYER NOTES
for a
NEW BEGINNING

Today, God's Word spoke this to me_____

_____

_____

_____

_____

_____

I will let go of_____

_____

_____

_____

_____

_____

I will begin by_____

_____

_____

_____

> ²³A man finds joy in giving
> an apt reply-and how good is
> a timely word!
>
> **Proverbs 15:23 (NIV)**

I have to chuckle when I read this suggestion because it is so true in the sense of "inconvenient times". One of my teens gets off work at midnight, comes into our bedroom (mind you our lights are out, and we're fighting to stay awake until he gets home), and guess what? He paces beside the bed and wants to talk. A little light bulb goes off in my head. "You're tired and sleepy, but your teen wants to talk for the first time this week… you'd better listen." So my husband and I turn our lamps on beside the bed, prop up on our pillows, and listen. We end up having a great conversation, and learn more about our son and his friends. He says goodnight, we turn out the lights, and sleep even better than we would have before our lively chat.

PRAYER NOTES
for a
NEW BEGINNING

Today, God's Word spoke this to me_____

_____

_____

_____

_____

I will let go of_____

_____

_____

_____

_____

I will begin by_____

_____

_____

_____

_____

²³Since all have sinned and are falling short of the honor and glory which God bestows and receives.

²⁴[All] are justified and made upright and in right standing with God, freely and gratuitously by His grace (His unmerited favor and mercy), through the redemption which is [provided] in Christ Jesus.

Romans 3:23-24 (AMP)

The one underlying theme that I see in parents raising their teens today is that mothers and fathers cannot admit their child's wrongdoings. It seems that the parents take this as a direct slap at their parenting by having to admit their child's mistakes. I am convinced that the best parent is the humble one. One who can readily admit their child's imperfections and is quick to forgive them. By refusing to believe the truth, you are fueling further misbehavior. Please take a moment right now and analyze your heart. Are you one who quickly admits your mistakes and asks for forgiveness? Or is this a rarity? If it's the latter, then please ask God to reveal your shortcomings. This will put you immediately on the road to restoration.

PRAYER NOTES
for a
NEW BEGINNING

Today, God's Word spoke this to me_____

_____

_____

_____

_____

I will let go of_____

_____

_____

_____

_____

I will begin by_____

_____

_____

_____

> ²⁶She opens her mouth with wisdom, And on her tongue is the law of kindness.
>
> **Proverbs 31:26 (NKJV)**

Parents, just because your teen is young in years does not mean that they lack wisdom. Not all wisdom is gained by experience. Our teens actually are very wise, but we had to go through a process of realizing that our teenagers actually could add valuable insight to many situations. Now, we include our teenagers on many important decisions. Their input not only helps us, but gives our teens a sense of self-worth and confidence far beyond what they experience elsewhere.

A word of advice - If your teen cannot express their opinion, they will stop listening to yours.

PRAYER NOTES
for a
NEW BEGINNING

Today, God's Word spoke this to me_____

_____

_____

_____

_____

I will let go of_____

_____

_____

_____

_____

I will begin by_____

_____

_____

_____

_____

²²Now that you have purified yourselves by obeying the truth so that you have sincere love for your brothers, love one another deeply, from the heart.

1 Peter 1:22 (NIV)

We've noticed over the years that certain houses become the "hang out" houses for sleepovers. If your house is not the popular place, then force a change in which your teen hosts some of these sleepovers. A sure-fire way to attract teens to your house is to first invite them. Second, feed them, especially large quantities of food for boys. Third, create a warm and fun environment which starts with you and your attitude. Love your teen's friends as though they are your own. In return, your home will be abundantly blessed with happy teens!

PRAYER NOTES
for a
NEW BEGINNING

Today, God's Word spoke this to me_____

_____

_____

_____

_____

I will let go of_____

_____

_____

_____

_____

I will begin by_____

_____

_____

_____

42. KEEP YOUR TEEN INVOLVED

⁴The sluggard craves and gets nothing, but the desires of the diligent are fully satisfied.

Proverbs 13:4 (NIV)

"Idle Hands are the Devil's Workshop"

Boredom is an extremely dangerous state of mind. Pay close attention to your child's interests and talents, so that you can steer them appropriately. If nothing stands out, then use trial and error. Begin by signing them up for music lessons, tennis lessons or anything else in which they may show interest.

With my teens I have used the trial and error technique successfully. My middle son has always been involved in sports, and never seemed passionate about his involvement. Because of our encouragement, he signed up at school for a guitar class, and absolutely loved it. I saw a passion burning in him that I have never seen before. So put your antennas up, and help plug your child into something they can excel in and enjoy.

PRAYER NOTES
for a
NEW BEGINNING

Today, God's Word spoke this to me_____

_____

_____

_____

_____

_____

I will let go of_____

_____

_____

_____

_____

_____

I will begin by_____

_____

_____

_____

_____

43. RESPECT YOUR TEEN

⁴**And now a word to you fathers. Don't make your children angry by the way you treat them. Rather, bring them up with the discipline and instruction approved by the Lord.**

Ephesians 6:4 (NLT)

Our oldest son, who is almost out of the teenage years, will be getting married soon. We wanted to spend our last Spring Break before he married as a family. He agreed to spend the break with us. A couple of days ago, he called and asked to go with his buddies on a cheap cruise instead. Initially, I was hurt and sad that he didn't want to spend the time with his family. My first inclination was to say "No, absolutely not. How could you consider not being with us?" But within a couple of minutes, I put "myself" aside and thought of him only and his future. I knew that he would be a young husband, and probably never have the opportunity to take a cruise with his friends again; whereas, he would have many more Spring Breaks with us. I swallowed the lump in my throat, and gave him my blessing to go and have fun. He said "Thank you Mom, I love you so much." Ironically he ended up not going on the cruise (by his own choice), and brought his fiancé with us to the beach instead. Respect means, at times putting their desires above yours.

PRAYER NOTES
for a
NEW BEGINNING

Today, God's Word spoke this to me_____

_____

_____

_____

_____

I will let go of_____

_____

_____

_____

_____

I will begin by_____

_____

_____

_____

44. ROUTINELY SCHEDULE ONE-ON-ONE TIME WITH YOUR CHILD

> [17] As iron sharpens iron,
> So a man sharpens the
> countenance of his friend.
>
> **Proverbs 27:17** (NKJV)

Whether it's pizza in the park, playing home run derby, or simply sipping hot chocolate together on a cold day, we literally try to meet each of our children's individual needs by giving them quality time. The key here is to CARVE OUT one-on-one time with your child. It doesn't have to cost anything, but the rewards are priceless!!

PRAYER NOTES
for a
NEW BEGINNING

Today, God's Word spoke this to me_____

_____

_____

_____

_____

I will let go of_____

_____

_____

_____

_____

I will begin by_____

_____

_____

_____

_____

^{17}"Also, I set watchmen over you, saying, 'Listen to the sound of the trumpet!' But they said, 'We will not listen.'"

Jeremiah 6:17 (NKJV)

My teens have revealed to me that when they have sat with their friends at church, they have talked to each other, played games on their cell phones, and instant-messaged each other during the service. They indicated to us that sitting near or with us have kept their attention on the sermon, which ultimately resulted in them getting closer to the Lord. An alternative to them sitting with you could be you sitting a couple of rows behind them. You are giving your teen some freedom, but also keeping a watchful eye on them and ensuring they are paying attention.

PRAYER NOTES
for a
NEW BEGINNING

Today, God's Word spoke this to me_____

_____

_____

_____

_____

_____

I will let go of_____

_____

_____

_____

_____

_____

I will begin by_____

_____

_____

_____

46. BE HOME WHEN YOUR TEEN GETS HOME FROM SCHOOL OR WORK

³Don't be selfish; don't live to make a good impression on others. Be humble, thinking of others as better than yourself. ⁴Don't think only about your own affairs, but be interested in others, too, and what they are doing.

Philippians 2:3-4 (NLT)

This is the most important part of your teen's day. They walk in the door with their minds filled with stories, problems, and issues from their school day. They need a sounding board. Please, dear parent, if at all possible be that sounding board for your teen. If you work, try to change work shifts to be home when they get home. This also keeps your house filled with parental control rather than teen control.

My husband says I chisel at drawing out conversation with my children. I don't bore into their personal affairs, but simply stay interested and never stop asking. Granted, they resist at times, but I am a die-hard, and don't take "no" for an answer. My husband laughs at me, yet behind closed doors has said that he is amazed at the positive results I obtain.

101

PRAYER NOTES
for a
NEW BEGINNING

Today, God's Word spoke this to me_____

_____

_____

_____

_____

_____

I will let go of_____

_____

_____

_____

_____

_____

I will begin by_____

_____

_____

_____

⁴He must rule his own household well, keeping his children under control, with true dignity, commanding their respect in every way and keeping them respectful. ⁵For if a man does not know how to rule his own household, how is he to take care of the church of God?

1 Timothy 3:4-5 (AMP)

At one time, I ran a home-based business plus I was active in numerous volunteer jobs.

Between the telephone calls, meetings and frequent visitors, my relationship with God, my husband and my children suffered. Luckily, my eyes were opened quickly and I stepped down from the volunteer work and closed my business (which was flourishing) so that I could re-establish my priorities. I am extremely thankful that God gave me the wisdom to make these two important decisions. I've never regretted it for a second. I now see parents over-extending, leaving their families on the sidelines and damage being done. I am not telling you to quit your job. If you have to work, then keep everything else to a minimum. God first, family second, everything else third.

PRAYER NOTES
for a
NEW BEGINNING

Today, God's Word spoke this to me_____

_____

_____

_____

_____

I will let go of_____

_____

_____

_____

_____

I will begin by_____

_____

_____

_____

*¹⁷Discipline your son,
and he will give you peace;
he will bring delight to your soul.*

Proverbs 29:17 (NIV)

There is a fine line between placing your teen in a safe secure "box" and putting them in "jail". Being too strict could cause them to rebel. Conversely, if you are too lenient, you risk losing them to the intense pressures of adolescence.

My experience raising three teenagers has taught me that they are most comfortable when I am consistently firm in my discipline. Remember, your teen is still your child, and in reality, they are not prepared to make adult decisions. Even though they might express anger and resentment at your correction, deep down your child takes comfort in your leadership. So step up to the plate and be their parent, which means setting reasonable standards and enforcing them.

PRAYER NOTES
for a
NEW BEGINNING

Today, God's Word spoke this to me_____

_____

_____

_____

_____

I will let go of_____

_____

_____

_____

_____

I will begin by_____

_____

_____

_____

> ^{26}The godly give good advice to their friends; the wicked lead them astray.
>
> **Proverbs 12:26 (NLT)**

We purposely plan activities at our home just to meet and spend time with our teen's friends. Become proficient at something your teenager loves to do. Whether it's tennis, ping-pong, playing card games, or watching sports with them, having common interests with your teens opens a door for you to communicate with them and their friends. You will find that, communication brings about awareness.

PRAYER NOTES
for a
NEW BEGINNING

Today, God's Word spoke this to me_____

_____

_____

_____

_____

I will let go of_____

_____

_____

_____

_____

I will begin by_____

_____

_____

_____

50. ENCOURAGE, ENCOURAGE, ENCOURAGE

> [11]Therefore encourage one another
> and build each other up,
> just as in fact you are doing.
>
> 1 Thessalonians 5:11 (NIV)

Please make a conscious effort to notice the good things in your child and verbalize it to them. For example, my 17-year-old son is taking guitar lessons for the first time and last night he played me a song from my era and I was so overwhelmed at how accomplished he had become in such a short period that I started tearing up. Immediately, I took this opportunity to let him know how awesome he sounded and how it touched my heart to see him passionate about something he's never attempted before. In summary, please don't hide your emotions. Make a concerted effort to let them know how valuable they are, both in their successes and in their failures. Daily exhort your child.

Titles by
June H. Olin

Rx for Happiness
Rx for Healing
Rx for Raising Teens

Watch for these upcoming titles:

Rx for Letting Go
Rx for Overcoming Fear
Rx for Financial Prosperity
Rx for Weight Control

For more information on ordering these books, write to:

Rx Books
PMB120
2020 Fieldstone Pkwy, Suite 900
Franklin, Tennessee 37069

Or e-mail Info@Rxbooks.com
www.Rxbooks.com